Pssst...Means
I Love You

Pamela Morey

Illustrations by Jennifer Rain Crosby

Balboa Press books may be ordered through booksellers or by contacting:

Balboa Press
A Division of Hay House
1663 Liberty Drive
Bloomington, IN 47403
www.balboapress.com
1 (877) 407-4847

The views expressed in this work are solely those of the author and do not necessarily reflect the views of the publisher, and the publisher hereby disclaims any responsibility for them.

ISBN: 978-1-9822-2873-6 (sc)
ISBN: 978-1-9822-2874-3 (e)

Library of Congress Control Number: 2019906912

Print information available on the last page.

Balboa Press rev. date: 06/24/2019

BALBOA
PRESS
A DIVISION OF HAY HOUSE

With Love always to
Graham Griffin Giordan & Melina

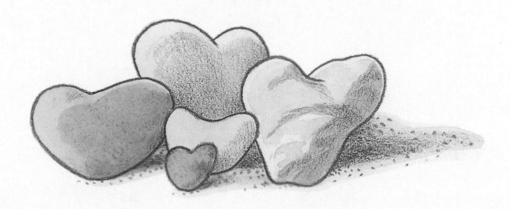

Morning Love

In the morning when I wake up I have a
favorite way to start my day!

My mommy or daddy and I like to share some "Morning Love"

We like to start our day with a big hug & kiss and "I Love You"

I feel so happy and loved when I start my day like this

I feel good and know I will have a great day!

Pssst...Means I Love You!

My family & I have a secret, it is our own
way of saying something special.

Our special word is "Pssst" ...and it means
"I love you"

My mommy likes to surprise me with a **Pssst**
When she sees me playing nicely and having fun.

My daddy says "Pssst" to me when he sees me being kind & helpful to others. Sometimes they say "Pssst" for no reason at all.

I like to say "Pssst" to mommy and daddy too; it's a nice way to let them know I appreciate them, and I know it makes them happy.

Family Hugs

One of our favorite things to do with our family is to share a family hug.

We all huddle together and hug each other all
at once and shout "FAMILY HUGS!"

It is our way of saying "I love you" to each other all at once.

We feel so good when we share our family love...

and it makes me feel so warm and happy inside!

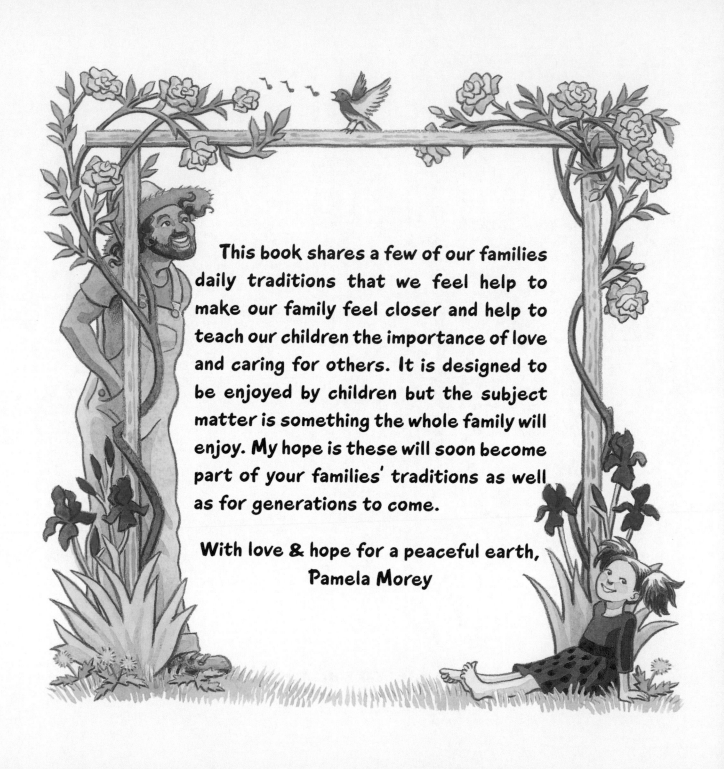

This book shares a few of our families daily traditions that we feel help to make our family feel closer and help to teach our children the importance of love and caring for others. It is designed to be enjoyed by children but the subject matter is something the whole family will enjoy. My hope is these will soon become part of your families' traditions as well as for generations to come.

With love & hope for a peaceful earth,
Pamela Morey

Printed in the United States
By Bookmasters